THE CHRISTIAN WAY

Keith Ward

THE CHRISTIAN WAY

LONDON
SPCK

First published 1976
SPCK
Holy Trinity Church
Marylebone Road
London NW1 4DU

BV
4501.2
.W337

Printed in Great Britain by
Bocardo and Church Army Press Ltd,
Cowley, Oxford

ISBN 0 281 02893 1

*To the people
of Hampstead Parish Church
who helped to show me
the way*

CONTENTS

1 FAITH

In all religions there is a relentless and continuing battle; it exists within the Christian churches as much as it exists anywhere else. Between the two parties joined in this battle there is a fundamental and decisive conflict. The conflict is between those who accept religion as a liberating, life-enhancing, creative exploration of existence; and those who turn to religion as a safe, secure, dogmatic, infallible system of beliefs and practices, adherence to which clearly separates its devotees from all other men and gives them an exclusive monopoly of truth which no one else can share.

Of all the many differences between religions and the various sects of religion, this is the most decisive and fundamental division. It is embedded in the very heart of the Christian religion from the beginning. Whereas the letter to the Colossians speaks of putting on the new nature of compassion, kindness, humility, gentleness, patience, forbearance, forgiveness, and love (Col. 3. 2-15), the letter to Titus tells believers to warn heretics twice, then cast them out (Titus 3. 11); and the first letter to the Corinthians warns believers not even to eat with drunks or slanderers (1 Cor. 5. 9-13). The same gospel which preaches unlimited love for all men also carries within it the seeds of exclusivism and intolerance, which is concerned with the correctness of doctrine among believers and the exclusion of outsiders, to be consigned to Satan for the destruction of the body (2 Cor. 5. 1-5). It may be thought that my selection of texts in isolation is unfair, and I am not saying that these texts are themselves intolerant; we need to examine their contexts much more carefully before we could come to that conclusion. Nevertheless, it is undoubted that they have been used as a basis for intolerant attitudes by later groups of Christians.

This strange mixture of unlimited love and harsh intolerance is characteristic of every religious institution. The battle for love is never finally won against the forces of intolerance. Until this is seen, the complex nature of religious belief has not been fully grasped. On the one hand, religion is the creative pursuit of love and fulfilment. On the other hand, religion is the dogmatic and restrictive systematization of exclusive dogmas and practices which divide the saved elect clearly from the damned outsiders. Creative religion and restrictive religion are the two opposed faces of the same human phenomenon.

In face of this fundamental conflict, the many disputes which take place within religion — disputes about Catholic versus Protestant, ritual versus free prayer, Bishops versus Presbyters, Latin or Elizabethan English versus modern English — are of relative insignificance. Indeed, they are usually disputes which take place within two forms of restrictive religion. The disputants agree that religion is a destructive and divisive force in human life; and they show this by their violent and abusive language. They do not seek tolerant understanding and constructive growth in unity. Instead, they harden their views into mutually opposed factions and seek to hurt and destroy their opponents — all in the name of a religion of love.

Restrictive religion can be seen in the many wars and cruel tortures imposed throughout history in the name of religion. Restrictive religion is the enemy of love and of creative religion, which it always seeks to absorb and destroy.

The battle between creative and restrictive religion is not a battle which is fought out in other people or other churches. It is fought out in ourselves. Every religious believer has part of himself which tends to be enslaved by restrictive religion; creativity has to be fought for and defended at all times; and there are many insidious traps which can turn one from achieving it, even when one thinks the battle won in oneself. The only hope of winning is to bring the enemy out in the open, identify it clearly and stamp it out in one's own life.

Of course, restrictive religion is not to be stamped out by violence, intolerance, or vehement argument; those are precisely the tools by which restrictive religion grows and flourishes. The only way of stamping out restrictivism is by the unswerving pursuit of love. This may lead to apparent defeat by the more powerful forces of restriction. But, like the defeat of the cross itself, out of such defeats God draws the real and enduring triumphs of faith.

How, then, can we identify creative faith? Its basic criterion is this: it must enable one to find fulfilment in one's life, to become a full and active human personality. What I here call 'fulfilment' is characterized in the Bible in many different ways — as liberation, redemption, salvation, reconciliation, healing. But it is clear throughout that what Christians seek is not just intellectual belief, but a faith which brings salvation. The Christian message is that one can find fulfilment (salvation) through faith. That word 'salvation' has the double meaning of liberating one from negative restrictions which confine our humanity,

11

and leading one to health, or wholeness. It is vital for the Christian to ensure that his faith really does free him from bondage, make him whole, and bring fulfilment; that it does not restrict or even harm and confine him.

On the Christian view, there are three important aspects of human fulfilment. First, whatever can be said to fulfil human life must use to the full those capacities which are central and proper to being human. Man was made in the image of God (Gen. 1. 27); and he must use the gifts God has given him, not leave them lying dormant (Luke 19. 12-27). There may be disputes about which capacities are central, and about how they can be properly used. But nothing can count as fulfilment unless it does use those capacities which we take to be central to human nature, or to be our own special gift. Second, that which fulfils human nature must bring happiness or contentment; nothing which brings only misery and mental anxiety can be called fulfilling. Jesus promised his followers a joy which would be complete and which no man could take from them (John 15. 11), and the end of human life is eternal joy in God. Third, for anything to fulfil human nature it must be concerned with the building up of the social community within which alone man, as an essentially social animal, can flourish fully. There is room for disagreement about the exact sort of relationship man should take to his community. But one can accept that fulfilment must lie in some form of positive relationship to one's fellows. As Paul writes, we should aspire to excel in those things which build up the church community (1 Cor. 14. 12), and in Acts 2. 42 we read that the first believers shared the common life with joy. The Christian believes that fulfilment —

except for the special case of those with a contemplative vocation — must be found within a community of love, and must share in and build up such a community.

Restrictive religion is not concerned with this sort of fulfilment. For religion can stunt and limit the exercise of many human capacities. The legacy of Puritanism in Britain has sometimes been a negative and legalistic attitude which has led to the destruction of many art treasures; and sometimes, in the name of Christianity, whole libraries have been burnt and destroyed. Again, mournful processions of people dressed in black, whipping themselves and doing penance, are a strange way of bringing happiness to mankind. The 'priests in black gowns' decried by William Blake seem a very far cry from that spirit of joy and overwhelming happiness of which the New Testament letters speak. And as for love, it is undeniable that many deeds committed in the name of religion have been degrading and morally perverse, from the tortures of the Inquisition to the wars of the Crusades.

In face of all these terrible aberrations, it is natural enough to draw back from religion altogether and oppose it as the enemy of humanitarian progress. At such a point, one must remember that a basic goal of the religious life is fulfilment, true humanization; and whatever opposes such fulfilment must be thrown aside, however 'religious' in the restrictive sense it may seem to be. It is salutary to remember that some forms of religion are restrictive and even demonic; and to recall that it was pious religious believers who crucified Jesus of Nazareth, because he was a heretic and a trouble-maker. Jesus is the hero of creative faith; he is remembered as one in whom humanity

13

was completely fulfilled, and as one who was rejected and killed by religion.

Creative faith, then, stands for the full and proper use of central human capacities, for happiness and for the commitment to love of others. But it is always threatened by restrictive faith. And so one must constantly be on one's guard and ask oneself what, in one's own life and in the life of one's religious community, is conducive to human fulfilment; what is irrelevant to fulfilment; and what may actually oppose or hinder it. The religious life, as we know it, remains a continuing battle; not a battle between religion and irreligion, but between the faith which kills and the faith which brings life and joy. It is therefore not enough to hold the Christian faith; we must be sure that our faith makes us free men (Gal. 5. 13), that it sets our feet upon the path of life (Rom. 6. 4), that it brings us to mature manhood, measured by nothing less than the full stature of Christ (Eph. 4. 13), that it brings us to fulfilment in love.

2 FULFILMENT

Has the search for fulfilment anything essentially to do with religion? It may be said that such a search is a purely humanist affair; far from being a central question of religion, it must be of merely peripheral importance. What is central to religion, it may be held, is true belief about the existence of supernatural beings, or worship of such beings in a manner which is believed to be acceptable. If one has the right beliefs and performs the correct devotional acts, one has religion; whether or not one finds fulfilment is quite a distinct matter. This view of religion seems to me about as wrong as it can be; and it is also extremely naive in neglecting the way in which belief in God and adoration of God, properly understood, are matters which involve the human heart totally, requiring a transformation of mind and a re-orientation of life. One does not come to believe in God in the way a scientist might dispassionately come to believe in sub-atomic particles; one finds oneself being involved in a changing and hesitant dialogue of love with a reality and will beyond one's own. And one does not worship God adequately by performing so many ritual acts; one responds in love to the call of a love beyond one's own, and with a love which grows from within and beyond the bounds of one's conscious personality. So even to believe in and adore God rightly is to begin to explore that love in which ultimate human fulfilment is found; belief and worship cannot be divorced from fulfilment. If they are divorced, one has simply not got true belief and devotion.

The biblical record is quite clear on this point. If a man knows all the truths there are to be known about God, his nature and his actions, if he affirms all the Catholic creeds, but lives an unfulfilled, immoral, unhappy life, then his 'religious' faith is worth nothing (Cf. 1 Cor. 13). Jesus came to give life, light, healing, wholeness, and liberation to the human person, too often enslaved by sin. A faith which rests on the assertion that God became man cannot be accused of neglecting that which brings human nature to its fulfilment, as it was in Christ. So a central religious question is, 'What must I do to be saved?', to be fulfilled. There are, of course, true and false beliefs in religion; but without the search for and attainment of fulfilment, all the rest is, in the end, ineffectual.

The implication of this is that if a man really strives for fulfilment he must be welcomed with love, whether he is a Hindu, humanist, or Marxist. Conversely, if a man has all the orthodox Christian beliefs about God and has not love, he must be pitied as a man who has not seen what faith is about. The character of faith is to be known by its fruits (Matt. 7. 16); and the fruits of an adequate faith are 'love, joy, peace, patience, kindness, goodness, fidelity, gentleness, and self-control' (Gal. 5. 22). These are the fruits of fulfilment, and they are the tests of genuine Christian faith.

Those fruits may be shared by non-Christians; but Christian believers will naturally think that non-Christians will not, in the end, attain lasting fulfilment — 'eternal life' — solely by the way they choose to follow. That is because Christians do think that final fulfilment must lie in the clear vision of God, by union with Christ. But that final fulfilment is a long way off — for all of us, Christians and non-Christians alike. In the meanwhile, humanism, for example, may fulfil a man more than the sort of Christianity he understands would; more, even, than the sort of Christianity we understand fulfils us. What we need above all — and what Christians have often tragically lacked — is humility and tolerance. Humility, to see that our understanding of Christianity may be a stumbling-block to others and even to our own fulfilment. Tolerance, to see the obvious truth that, here and now, many non-Christians do find a greater fulfilment in their different way than we do in our Christian way, however impeccably orthodox.

The believer in God, then, will say that true, final fulfilment lies in the knowledge and love of God; therefore the search for fulfilment is an essentially religious search. But he will be careful to add that he says this on faith, not because of his own attainment or because of some clearly false theory that only Christians produce fulfilled, holy people. And, because of the complexity of our present world, it is apparently true that some people find fulfilment better in non-religious ways. No doubt this is because they see only the restrictive face of religion; and perhaps we ourselves bear some responsibility for this. The fulfilment we should find in our faith is not always entirely obvious to others.

In saying that a central concern of faith is with fulfilment, there is no intention of fitting everyone into one predetermined pattern of faith. It would be restrictive and wrong to insist that each person must be fulfilled in only one way — by joining a house-group or communicating daily, for instance. People may be happy or depressed, healthy or ill, quiet and introspective, or friendly and boisterous. Whatever

17

their temperaments or whatever their situation in life, creative religion will try to accept them as they are and encourage them to find fulfilment in their own unique way. In other words, creative religion will never say, 'You must do it this way; you must believe exactly this; or else you are excluded and inferior or without hope.' What it will say is this: 'We have a fulfilment, a happiness, and a love which overwhelms us so much that we want to tell you about it. We will be glad to offer our help, advice, and encouragement. Moreover, we believe that this way is founded on a disclosure of the ultimate truth about reality, upon a command of God and a promise of fulfilment in obeying it. But you may not share this disclosure or may understand it differently. So you must seek fulfilment in your own way, not necessarily in the way we like.'

Yet a doubt may remain. Is all this concern for fulfilment not somehow self-centred and so immoral? Should we not rather be concerned with helping others first, or with discovering the truth about the world? Isn't it just a little too cosy and introverted to put fulfilment first? Some people feel this reservation very keenly. There are so many wrongs in the world to be put right that they think we should be actively putting them right, even at the cost of our own fulfilment. But it should be clear that loving concern for others is an essential part of religious fulfilment; to deny that is to fall into one of the traps of restrictive religion. Furthermore, to aim at fulfilment is not selfish in a bad sense. For it is not putting one's own whims and desires first, whatever others may want. It is simply trying to be a complete, liberated, creative human being; and the person who does not really want that for himself is not morally superior; he is almost incomprehensible. It should be noted that there is no intention of saying that one's own fulfilment must take up the whole of one's time, leaving no room for any other pursuits in life. That would be silly. One is simply saying that the pursuit of fulfilment is reasonable and important, and that it is a primary task of creative faith. There is nothing wrong with that. And though you might say that a man should devote a lot of his time to other things than religion, one must also bear in mind that, if fulfilment is even partially found, it will transform the whole of one's life, not just some narrow religious part of life. One will serve others with a new zeal, do everything one does with a new zest, and be capable of many more creative pursuits of all kinds, precisely because of one's faith. There is, after all, something rather sad about a man who devotes his life to putting the world right, when his own personal life is frustrated, sad, and in a general mess. There is nothing wrong with his trying to do good. But he might do better to devote some of his time to finding happiness and love in his own life; and then he would really have something worthwhile to give to others. Naturally, there are situations in which love of others conflicts with personal happiness; and then one cannot achieve complete fulfilment. But in general and for much of the time it is possible to pursue both and to exercise one's distinctive talents in doing so. I am not saying, then, that one should do nothing else than be religious — far from it. I am saying that if one gives some time to the religious quest — and that will require self-discipline, tenacity, and resolution — what one finds there will flow out through the whole of life, transforming its quality from beginning to end.

So a basic concern of creative religion is with human fulfilment. To believe is to participate in a community where such fulfilment is sought and found in different ways, by very different sorts of people. Religious faith is not the acceptance of a set of dogmatic propositions, intolerantly and exclusively defended. It is the pursuit of a renewed life, sought and disclosed in a community of those who desire the creative use of their human capacities, lasting happiness, and the power to love others in active goodness. It is the acceptance of the discipline — in time, reading, thought, and prayer — which is necessary to attain any worthwhile goal, and most especially the basic goal of human life itself, fulfilment. Creative religion begins with this search, the search for true humanity, for human fulfilment.

ALMIGHTY GOD,

you created us in your likeness, so that our lives may be an image of your eternal love;

you hold us in existence, so that we may grow into the fulness of being you intend for us;

you renew us by your presence, so that our life may be infused with your creative power.

Lord God, you are the creator of everything that is;

Grant us a share in your creative power; the wisdom to recognize the gifts you have given us; the strength and tenacity to use them to the full; the skill and sensitivity to apply them properly and well. Lord God, in your being is the awareness of eternal joy;

Grant us a share in your joy, as we delight in your creation and in your presence.

Lord God, in your being is the fulness of love;

Grant us a share in your love, as we respond to you and to your creation.

Lord, by your power make us free men; set our feet on the path of life; and bring us to the maturity of that true humanity which is found in Jesus Christ.

The Christian faith proclaims that fulfilment is to be found in the knowledge and love of God. The highest use of the creative powers of humanity, the truest happiness, and the greatest power to love are to be found when one submits oneself to a supremely valuable reality outside oneself. It is in open and creative response to such a reality, the Christian says, that fulfilment is to be found. And it is this that basically divides the believer from the unbeliever. The unbeliever either finds nothing valuable to respond to; or he does not respond at all; or, if he does respond, he does not do so creatively and fully, with all his being. The believer, on the other hand, seeks continually, throughout the whole of his life, to respond fully and creatively to the values which he discerns in objective reality and to the underlying source of all values which they may disclose, whatever his own personal circumstances. Such continual creative response is what is properly called 'faith'.

Fulfilment, then, is to be found in faith, in the adoption of a certain sort of attitude towards one's experience. But that is not an individualistic or subjective thing. Faith grows and flourishes only in community, in a fellowship of people who feel called to pursue fulfilment and help one another to find it; and our own idiosyncrasies can be corrected by a sympathetic understanding of the experiences of others. The attitude of faith develops in response to a reality which evokes it, the reality of God, who is apprehended within the Christian community as acting and offering himself supremely in Christ. Faith is a response within a community to the reality which offers complete fulfilment, the reality of God.

What is this response of faith which Christians proclaim? Throughout the New Testament, which is the record of the faith of the early church, aroused by response to Jesus and the proclamation of his resurrection, one can find the structure of faith outlined, the sort of response to God in which fulfilment is to be found. Again and again the same terms recur — joy, hope, peace, love, faith, wisdom, temperance — as characteristic of the sort of people Christians become when they have faith. These attitudes may be arranged under three basic characteristics of the life of faith — reverence, penitence, and love. The pattern of both private and liturgical prayer in the church has always followed this basic structure. Reverence includes adoration, gratitude, and humility — the response to a vision of the majesty and love of God as Creator. Penitence includes the wisdom which brings self-knowledge and self-control, faith, hope, and the joy of forgiveness — a response to the vision of the failure of man and the compassion of God. Love includes sympathy, justice, and the reconciliation of men to each other within the Christian community — the response to the redemptive activity of God reconciling men to each other and to himself. These three elements together make up the life of faith, of response to the reality of God as it is apprehended within the tradition of the Christian church.

These attitudes do not arise of their own accord and just in response to our own personal and maybe idiosyncratic experiences. They arise as a response to the disclosure of the character of God which is held to have been revealed in the person and work of Jesus. The community of the church was founded on

23

that disclosure; and it continues to live by seeking to arouse the same response to that disclosure, as it has been recorded in the Scriptures and as it is proclaimed in word and sacrament, week by week. There is a disclosure, a revelation, given to and preserved by this community. That is why the Christian faith is a gospel, good news that God has acted to reveal himself, rather than a systematic doctrine thought up by some sage. It is in this sense that the 'foolishness of the cross' is quite distinct from the 'wisdom of the Greeks' (1 Cor. 1. 22-24). The Christian community merely testifies to God's self-revelation in Christ; it does not primarily teach a systematic philosophy or theology. It is the character of God which is disclosed, not a set of intellectual propositions or definitions; and it is that which the church tries to preserve in its use of the Bible. So what it calls for from us is not primarily an intellectual assent, but more basically a creative response of self-commitment to the attitudes which are a natural reaction to the appreciation of God's initiative in unveiling his being.

This means that the Christian way is a specific revelation given to a specific community, which, we believe, declares the character and purposes of God in a definitive way. In that respect, it is unalterable and unique. God may have, and undoubtedly has, disclosed himself in other ways to other communities. But where there are differences of attitude and doctrine, the Christian naturally believes that the way of Christ gives the most adequate picture of God. We must allow others to follow the ways they accept; but it is illogical to say that we believe their ways to be just as good in all respects as ours; for the plain fact is that these ways are often incompatible in what they declare. The difficult task for the Christian is to

24

stand for the truth as he sees it without being unduly restrictive or intolerant of the opinions of others. This requires of him that he should constantly recall and seek to preserve the vision which called him to Christian commitment; and that he should constantly attempt to deepen his response of reverence and love. If he does this, he will be both aware of the limitations of his own vision and open through sympathetic concern to appreciate the insights and efforts of others.

Even within Christianity, some people are by nature conservative, will tend to accept all the biblical records as literally true and hold a definite and fairly precise, detailed view of the nature and destiny of man as revealed therein. Other people are by nature radical and will tend to have a more critical approach to the biblical literature, to be agnostic about a great many matters, and to prize freedom of inquiry and action more highly. Both sorts of people — and maybe most of us lie between these extremes — may build up their lives on reverence, penitence, and love, in response to what is disclosed to them in Christ and in communion with the Christian community. Their differences should thus be seen as legitimate and permissible, as long as they put first what is most important — the pursuit of the love of God, in the way of Christ in which they share.

Conservatives and radicals can learn much from each other if they sincerely try to grow together in a loving, sharing community. For each has temptations — one applies too easily and rigorously rules which belong to a different age, and the other throws out too readily passages which he finds awkward — which discussion can help to alleviate. It is not easy to start such discussion and to prevent it from becoming divisive. But Christians are called to do this, prayerfully, and so learn from each other. The present disunity of the church is perhaps largely the result of intolerance and intransigence, which so easily seems to characterize the Christian religion as it gains power and prestige. We should learn humility from our disunity, and the desire to grow together again, as we put love first (1 Cor. 13). Intellectual tolerance must be combined with absolute commitment to the spiritual life before a balanced and united Christian church can once again exist.

This is not a plea for the acceptance of a liberal theology. It is a plea to conservatives and liberals alike to put the love of God first and to accept the fact of intellectual disagreement as what it is, a symptom of human divergence in temperament and ways of seeing the world, which does not necessarily preclude men from coming together to share in the community which celebrates and perpetuates the disclosure of God found in Christ, and brings us to liberation and fulfilment through our loving response to that disclosure.

Fulfilment, then, is found in creative response to the vision of God which is celebrated within the Christian community. 'Where there is no vision, the people perish' (Prov. 29. 18); and to enter into and continue within the Christian way, one needs consstantly to renew the Christian vision. To renew ourselves and our inner lives, to achieve fulfilment as truly human beings, it is not enough to obey the rules or to believe the correct things. We must return to the source of Christian life in the vision of God which comes to us through Christ. That vision is dramatically expressed in the New Testament and offered in the preaching and sacraments of the church. It may come to us, as individuals, in many different forms and at unexpected times. But to enter onto the Christian way, the way of eternal life, one must begin by making oneself open to that vision, however and whenever it will come; and one must continue by remaining true to it, whatever subsequently happens to us. To prepare oneself for vision, to reanimate such moments of vision, is the task of prayer. The community of Christian people is the fellowship of those who wait for the vision of God, who celebrate it, and who seek to make it present to one another. Our fulfilment is in the fulness of that vision of which we now have a foretaste in our response to the living Christ.

ALMIGHTY GOD,

We await the vision of your glory; help us in our darkness by leading us to light; help us in our ignorance by leading us to knowledge; help us in our solitude by leading us to the fellowship of your love.

Lord, we celebrate the vision of your love which we have seen in the face of Jesus, and we thank you for the life which you give us as we look to you.

Help us to become what we love, so that we may live the life of Christ.

Help us to show this life to others, that the vision which we see may also be seen through us; that the love we receive we may give to others.

Grant us the vision of your presence, Lord; renew our life by your love.

4 WORSHIP

The first basic attitude characteristic of the Christian response to the vision of God is worship; and in developing that attitude the vision itself becomes clearer and firmer. To believe in God is ideally to worship at all times. For worship is not something that one only does in certain holy places or at certain holy times. As the word suggests, to worship is to ascribe worth. It is not to say, 'How good and marvellous you are', like a sycophantic courtier. It is not to say anything in particular. It is just to contemplate with appreciation the worth of what lies before one. Worship lies not in the words one says, but in the natural response of one's mind to value or worth.

It seems, then, that one may worship anything of value. If anything truly has value, if we take the time and trouble to contemplate it with care and love, that is a form of worship. To worship is to allow the mind to rest in the loving contemplation of what is really good and valuable.

May we, then, worship good people, beautiful scenery, or even the crown jewels? Indeed we may. In the 1662 marriage service of the Church of England, the man promises, 'with my body I thee worship'. We worship a person when we grant them their true worth; and this granting of worth may be expressed either simply in a mental attitude of appreciation or, if the opportunity offers, in appropriate action, like treating with care and tenderness and preserving from harm. The Christian should be a person who worships, in attitude and action, every person and thing and situation which is of value, in the way and to the degree that such contemplative or active reverence is appropriate.

It is most important to see that if one does not worship all things, insofar as they have worth, one cannot really be worshipping God at all. There are people who spend much time in church or saying prayers, but who never take time to contemplate reverently the things and people of the ordinary everyday world, just to see them as they really are. To perceive things rightly, appreciate them fully, and respond to them appropriately, is a necessary part of the worship of God. And many of us can begin to understand what it means to worship God by first of all learning to worship beautiful and valuable things and persons; to value them for themselves and not for what they can do to help or interest us.

Indeed, for most of us, most of the time, God is known precisely through those things which we worship in everyday life; he is known in and through the persons and situations we meet. In this sense, as Iris Murdoch has put it, worship consists in the cultivation of a 'pure delight in the independent existence of what is excellent' (*The Sovereignty of the Good*, p. 85). But of course the Christian believes that such reverent contemplation will not only reveal things themselves in their finitude; they may also become transparent to a limitless and sustaining reality lying beyond them. When we catch a glimpse of the mystery and wonder of the universe, when we catch ourselves marvelling at the sheer fact that it exists at all, then we come near to one further strand of worship. When we sense the immense creative power which underlies all things, then we begin to see more of what it is to worship. When we find ourselves overwhelmed by a love and delight which seems to go beyond the physical objects we are looking at to some invisible source, then we begin to feel another depth of worship. To begin to sense this mystery, awe, and love is to begin to appreciate the quality of worship in its fulness. Many of us catch glimpses of such experiences from time to time, and then we see how a sense of awe enters into worship as we catch a glimpse of the alien yet fascinating reality which is beyond all the finite values we worship in our more everyday experiences, but which is known through them and demands our unreserved commitment.

So we can best learn to worship God by worshipping finite things rightly; by taking time to be quiet and rest in beauty for its own sake; by seeking to let things speak of what is beyond but lets itself be known through them. Worship is not saying, 'O God, you are very great; well done.' It is setting ourselves to see and respond to the value in all things; and to submit ourselves to a reality of absolute value if and when it shows itself in our experience. Our part is to open the mind to see clearly, to free the heart to feel appropriately, and to train the will to respond rightly. When and if we have done our part, it is for God to reveal himself to us in our lives in his own way. Worship is, then, a general attitude or mood, a readiness and determination to see and celebrate value, wherever it is to be found. It is the simple and unreserved delight in being.

Worship is not only an attitude which looks forward in readiness to celebrate the future; it also involves gratitude for all the gifts of God. The Christian aim is to 'give thanks every day for every thing to our God and Father' (Eph. 5. 20); to receive every person and situation as God's gift, as ordered towards our final fulfilment. The theist will say that

31

this way of seeing his experience, a way in which one can train oneself to see better and more constantly, is entirely natural and unsurprising. It does not require some momentous 'leap of faith' beyond appearances to a hidden reality beyond. On the contrary, it requires a positive 'leap of unfaith' to deny the obvious propriety of such an attitude. Man by nature tends to see his experience in personalistic terms, in terms of constant interaction with a spiritual force or forces, and it requires sophistication to deny that this is the case.

The believer will say that as he trains his mind to be open to the possibility of such a reality, it becomes known to him as that which gives and orders his experiences. To be thankful at all times and in all places opens the mind to the personal reality from which all experiences derive; our gratitude opens up to us the presence of the ground and giver of our experiences, much as our love can open up to us the personality of another person. We adopt the attitudes of worship and thankfulness in the first place because they help us to make more of our daily lives, they help us to live at peace and more fully. They teach us to value what we encounter daily and to celebrate life without just taking it for granted. Thus they seem to be attitudes which are conducive to our fulfilment. Then, as we adopt them, we come to discern more and more elements of value and meaning in our experience, to see a reality shining through and a purpose at work in experience. At that stage, worship and thankfulness broaden out beyond the recognition and celebration of value and significance in finite things, to an acknowledgment of the personal reality which works through them, in its moment-by-moment encounter with us. Finally, we are able to enter into the creative relationship of love, in which worship and thankfulness are joined and we are united to the source of our being to reach fulfilment.

Worship also involves humility — not the grovelling self-depreciation to which humanists object, but the acceptance that we are at every moment of existence totally dependent for our being. We receive our existence and our talents as something given, to be used responsibly, but never completely at our disposal. Our life is given to us; and we worship by offering freely what has been given, and not clinging to or appropriating it to ourselves alone. Humility is the preparedness to give up ourselves, our status, ambitions, and possessions, so that we may be dependent upon nothing but God, that we may cling to nothing but him who made us and holds us in being, and to whom all things return.

Finally, for Christians there is a special way to learn what worship is. For the New Testament provides the picture of a man who, in his character of love, is a window into the very heart of God. By meditating on the incidents of his life in the Gospels, by coming to him in the sacrament, by offering ourselves to him and patterning our lives on his, we hope to become what we love. We see the vision of God in the face of Jesus; and that glory which we see, we ask him to give us, through our union with him. This is another way of adoration, to love the Christ whom we find in the Gospels, in the liturgy of the church, and within the Christian fellowship, this image of eternal love; and so to grow into his own love for all the world.

Worship, then, is the natural response of the mind to the vision of the being of God. In awe before the mysterious source of all things; in delight in the being of all good things; in gratitude for all the wonderful gifts of his love; in that humility which is prepared to offer freely what has been freely given; and in affectionate love for Christ, who shows the character of God to us; in all these ways the Christian learns to make adoration the constant, still centre of his daily living.

LORD, may we find in every moment a sacrament of your presence;

may we hear your call to care in every claim upon us;

may we receive each happiness and beauty as your gift of love.

May we seek you in the silence of our inward being and find your presence in the depths of our life; may adoration be the still centre of our life today.

Lord, we adore your mystery and majesty;

increase in us that sense of worship which takes time to discern and delight in all that is good;

increase in us that sense of thankfulness which receives each situation as a gift at your hands;

increase in us that true humility which seeks to adore you at all times; not to cling to what you give, but to use your gifts in your service.

Lord, you have made us to delight in your presence;

hallow our thoughts and wills that we may find our delight in you.

5 PENITENCE

The second dominant attitude of the Christian life is penitence. This is perhaps the most easily misunderstood part of the Christian life; and indeed, if it is considered in isolation, apart from worship and thankfulness, it can give rise to the impression that Christianity is unhealthily concerned with guilt and masochistic self-punishment. It is ironic that the faith which claims to liberate men from sin has sometimes seemed to induce in men a sense of sin and personal unworthiness which they had never felt hitherto.

Like worship and thanksgiving, penitence must be understood primarily as a general disposition, adopted throughout the whole of one's experience. It is the disposition always to examine one's own motives and intentions, to bring them to full consciousness, and to assess them by the standard of absolute love. And it is the constant acceptance of God's forgiveness, in faith. The religious quest is for a liberation from greed, anxiety, and fear into a life of creative happiness and love; and the major world religions all propound their own answers to the question of how to achieve such liberation. For instance, the Buddhist answer, at least in some forms, is one of renunciation. To escape the wheel of suffering all desire has to be renounced. This requires many lifetimes of hard and difficult renunciation and discipline. The ordinary lay-believer can hope for little more than to improve his position very slightly in the next reincarnation; release from suffering will come only after many lifetimes of effort.

This is not the Christian answer. The Christian

answer is that God freely justifies the man who turns to him through faith in Christ. This doctrine has led to many misconceptions. It has been thought that if a man is morally guilty and deserves to be punished, all he has to do is say, 'I believe that Jesus is the Son of God', and God will let him off scot-free. So one gets the old question, 'Why can't I have a good time now; and on my death-bed become a Christian, and so get away with it all?' Of course, it is not like that at all. Faith in Christ is not just a matter of being baptized or assenting to some intellectual statement. It is a sort of personal trusting, a personal relationship of commitment, which can stand through times of depression, trial, or difficulty, and which usually needs to be built up slowly and deeply. Justification is not just letting off a jail sentence, though it sounds rather like it. It is the real transformation of a man, so that he becomes the fulfilled person he was meant to be, through union with God. The man who trusts in Christ daily tries to crucify his sinful (unfulfilled) self, as Jesus was crucified on the cross, and to let Christ live in and through his own life. That is, there is more to it even than a personal relationship with God. There is an actual re-creation, so that one becomes transparent to God, one becomes the vehicle of God's own love.

There has occasionally been controversy between theologians about whether men are actually made just by God, or whether they are regarded as just, even though they remain sinners. A study of the lives of most Christians makes it obvious that all who have faith in Christ are not really at once creative and fulfilled human beings. Old faults remain; and all most of us can hope is that we are not now as bad as we would have been without Christ. The Christian hope is that we will be brought to fulfilment, by being perfectly united to Christ. We have this promise quite clearly from the moment of our baptism into the church. God promises that he will bring us to fulfilment, as long as we try sincerely to trust in him and be united to him.

Penitence remains an essential part of the Christian attitude, however, precisely because we never do achieve perfect fulfilment on earth. The most advanced of the saints are adamant that they too require penitence — the acknowledgement that they lead lives which have the natural consequences of sorrow, pain, and spiritual death. With this acknowledgement goes the recognition that we cannot of ourselves achieve fulfilment; that the whole world, and the part we play in the human drama, falls short of the community of love, peace, and righteousness which would be the fulfilling of God's will for men. This in turn leads to recognition of our need for the forgiveness and help of God. The penitent man is one who says, 'By the standard of love I fail; I can only rely wholly on God, that he may accept me and bring me to a fulfilment I cannot achieve alone.'

The meaning of God's forgiveness is not just that he lets us escape some penalty; it is that he accepts us, as we are, into full personal relationship with himself, if we acknowledge our failure and turn to him in trust. The attitude of repentance is not, therefore, one of anxiety, guilt-feelings, and continual gloom. That is penitence gone wrong, turned into a morbid, self-punishing depression; and that is itself a form of sin, of missing the mark of fulfilment, joy, and inner peace. The attitude of penitence involves clear self-examination, so that one recognizes one's own nature, with both its good qualities and its defects. It involves the realization that the consequences of one's actions are usually calculated to bring frustration, misery, and conflict both to oneself and to one's society. It involves the resolution to turn the will from these consequences, so that, even if one is unable to avoid such actions, one desires liberation from the condition which seems to enslave us and make them unavoidable. It involves the attempt to be totally reliant upon God, not upon our own moral efforts and resources. It involves the attempt to make one's life express God's love, power, and joy, rather than our own inadequacies and preconceived ideas.

God's forgiveness is not just some temporal act which he has to keep on repeating over and over again as we fall into the same vices over and over again. God's forgiveness is a constant disposition on the part of God to accept and unite us to himself, on the simple condition of recognition of sin, and turning from the consequences of sin by trusting in him and turning to him for his power. God's forgiveness is always there; when a minister declares absolution in church he simply declares what is always the case; all that is needed on our part is turning to God in trust.

The heart of penitence, then, is complete reliance upon God in one's daily living. This is really where the Christian answer to sin differs from, say, the traditional Buddhist answer. For the Buddhist, one must achieve one's own release, by arduous discipline and lifetimes of effort. But the Christian does not require complete renunciation of all desires; he wants to transform the world, not escape from it. And he turns to God in trust, to bring him to a fulfilment he cannot manage alone. Christians will say that they are redeemed by the death of Jesus on the cross. But it is not the physical shedding of blood which is, as it were, an entrance-ticket to heaven. It is that the life of God is offered to the final, uttermost point, so that men may come to fulfilment by partaking of that life. The Christian does not think of forgiveness in terms of death, suffering, and gloom, but in terms of life, risen, present, and available for him who will accept it. To turn in trust to a redeemer is not to ask someone else to do the work for us; it is to turn from our failure and self-concern to a liberating joy and life.

To escape the bondage of sin is to live creatively, lovingly, and with the joy of true happiness. It is better to think of and desire that ideal than to think gloomily of all the things one does wrong. The penitent man is one who is released from gloomy and anxious and self-despairing thoughts into the joy of knowing he is accepted and is being moulded into the image of Christ the eternal joy. Having assessed one's own negativity and joylessness, one's failure to live a positive, full human life, one simply lets go and lets God take over with his grace.

The grace of God is his love active towards us individually, releasing us from bondage and making us whole. It gives life and light and power; above all, it gives that joy which comes from the assurance that one is bound in love with God for ever. All we must do, on our part, is to start from faith — trust in God, tenacity in relying on his promises, obedience to his will. God does not love us because we do so many good things; nor can we win his love by greater moral effort. His love is given freely and unconditionally; and all we need to realize it in our lives is trusting faith in him. It is in that sense that our salvation is by faith, not works. God makes us whole by his unconditional love, which requires of us only our obedient response.

The joy of constantly renewed life is the mark of Christian penitence. The true penitent is the man who knows himself, who treasures an ideal of creative, loving, happy living, and who lives in God's power. He is a man whose life is marked especially by a deep and abiding joy. Christian penitence may begin with the recognition of failure; but its heart is the discovery of joy.

LORD, liberate us from attachment to the world; from the pride of possession and the fear of loss; from envy of others and from arrogance; from hypocrisy and from self-deceit;

Liberate us from indifference and contempt; from anxiety about ourselves and fear of the future; from timidity and obstinacy; from anger and intolerance;

Liberate us from misery and pain; from warfare and oppression; from famine and disease; from conflict and frustration;

Liberate us from all that impedes the fruition of creative happiness and love in our lives; from all that hinders peace and love in our society; from all that separates us from you;

Free us from all the desires and conventions that enslave us;

Save us from the ravages of greed and malice;

Heal the wounds of our pain and sorrow;

Bind us in the unity of your love;

Bring us to the fulfilment of our powers and make us whole;

Help us to know ourselves as we really are, to share with others in the gift of friendship, to find in our work a ready response to your calling and in our play an expression of the joy of life, to cherish the world as the gift of your creation and to find the fulness of joy in your presence.

Lord, you have made us in your image and for yourself;

may the love which the Spirit brings flood into our hearts

and unite us to you now and for ever.

The penitent man is one who lives in the power of God, whose life is filled with the Spirit of God. The Spirit is spoken of in the Old Testament as a source of wisdom, creativity, strength, leadership, and inspired utterance. The Spirit enabled Joseph to interpret Pharaoh's dream (Gen. 41. 38); Bezalel to be a master of design (Exod. 31. 3); made Moses the leader of his people (Num. 11. 17); caused prophetic ecstasy (Num. 11. 15); raised up judges and prophets (Judg. 3. 10), and was made known in many other great and mighty deeds done through God's servants. So the Spirit of God is seen as a power erupting like a mighty wind (the Hebrew word for Spirit is *ruāḥ*, breath or wind) at important moments of human life, strengthening and empowering a man's character.

The wind is invisible, it comes with power, it can destroy and tear down, it can refresh, it can invigorate, it is ever-changing. We can fight against it, but it can beat us down. We can be driven before it and be carried by its power. To open oneself to the Spirit is to be prepared to be beaten down but to hope to be refreshed and empowered. It is to allow one's life, one's hopes, one's plans to be shaped by its impelling force. It is dangerous and exhilarating. It is never to be taken lightly or faced with inadequate preparation and resolve. If we pray for the Spirit to come, we must be ready for either a cyclone or a gentle breeze, for a re-creation of ourselves. It is by constant obedience to the Spirit, as the continual source of our life at every moment, that the Christ-like character is formed in us by the Spirit.

By reliance on the Spirit, we can become vehicles of God's action in the world. Our own personality is not obliterated; it is, on the contrary, brought to new heights of creativity. But we can be conscious that we are vehicles of a power stemming from beyond, with which we co-operate and which we mediate. To turn to God fully is to be filled with the Spirit, to live in the experienced power of God. We still have to make decisions and efforts; we still fail and have to try again. But when we try, we are not trying to succeed by exerting our own strength. We are seeking to rely more perfectly on the power of the Spirit, subordinating our conscious ego to the power of God working through us.

Perhaps an analogy can be made with the experience of artists who are, as we say, inspired or 'taken over by the muse'. They do not cease to be individuals, and their art remains recognizably personal, yet in such moments it seems to spring from beyond the conscious self; one mediates rather than originates. What exactly results depends on one's character and training; but the source of creative power arises at depths beyond one's personal control.

The sort of attitude to which this leads in daily life is caught very well in the Zen aphorism, 'Let go and let God'. We must stop struggling and striving and being anxious about the course of our own lives, and simply allow God to work in us by the power of his life-giving Spirit.

I do not think the experience of the indwelling Spirit is a special gift; some such experience is the birthright of all Christians. But it may come to different people in different ways. Some have an instantaneous experience of the Spirit as a powerful, sudden force. But for others the Spirit is more like the pervasive rustling in the air which refreshes quietly and remains a constant, almost unnoticed presence. We should not expect any particular sort of experience in advance or be envious of those who seem to have a more overwhelming experience. The important thing, after all, is that we should daily seek to put our own ambitions and desires and fears at God's disposal, to rest quietly in whatever strength he gives, and to wait for his leading. He will not speak to all in the same way; but he will speak to all who ask, though he may do so quietly and subtly, and those whose lives are being gradually transformed may scarcely notice the change. God's strength is there in many different ways. Our task is simply to put our lives at his disposal as completely as we can, to let Christ come to birth in our lives, so that we can say with Paul, 'The life I now live is not my life, but the life which Christ lives in me' (Gal. 2. 20).

But what if there is no noticeable change in our lives? If we remain as loveless, greedy, and selfish as before? Here we must recall our Lord's command not to judge others or even ourselves. We are promised that faith is enough; and if we remember that faith does mean the sincere attempt to trust God and to let him control our lives, then we can be sure that God will make his will known in us sooner or later. It may not be for us to say when or how. What God begins to work in us may be obscured to others by great faults in our temperament or circumstances. There are those great saints in whom God does illustrate a great and dramatic power, but many of us do go on with fairly commonplace lives and fairly obvious flaws of character. It is just because of this that penitence is required of us; and I think that in the end one can only say that as we do try, in our own half-hearted way, to live the Christian life, there is in us at least the beginnings of that conformity to the Christ-life which is the destiny of each of us. And we must remember that we have eternity to complete this pilgrimage, the infinite resources of God to help us, and the sure promise of God that he will bring us to himself. So maybe we should not worry too much about the lack of dramatic change in our lives; we should leave that to God and concentrate solely on perfecting our faith, our trust and submission. That, I think, is very near the heart of the Christian gospel. Christ came to save sinners; in our sins, we must turn to him in faith, and he will begin to unite us to himself.

It may be thought that such a subordination of the conscious, rational self to a largely unknown, unpredictable force beyond is a dangerous thing; and of course it does have dangers. Judaism and Christianity have always recognized that there are evil spirits as well as good, that a man may be possessed by powers of evil as well as by God's Holy Spirit. That does not mean that we must not turn to the Spirit; for the man who tries to live his life solely on the level of rational, calculating thought misses the deepest sources of human life and creativity. He may miss also the deepest perversions of the human spirit; but it does not follow that because a course of life is the most innocuous, it is therefore the best one to follow. What we must try to do is to be fully aware of the powers of evil which so easily beset us and ensure that we do not give our lives to them. This we can do in two main ways. First, by constantly asking whether the Spirit that works in us is producing the fruits of the Spirit, 'Love, joy, peace, patience, kindness, goodness, fidelity, gentleness, and temperance' (Gal. 5. 22). And second, whether it does build up the community of those who are seeking to do God's will and reconcile men to one another. These are the tests by which we must 'test the spirits, to see whether they are from God' (1 John 4. 1).

The attitude of penitence, then, must always be considered in the wider context of the other attitudes which go to make up the Christian life — attitudes of worship, thankfulness, joy, and hope. And it has three main aspects. First, the clear examination of one's own life and character, so that one is able to see oneself as one is. Second, the realization of the consequences of that life as destructive of happiness, love, and creativity in oneself and of harmony, justice, and peace in one's community, so that one turns one's will from those consequences and desires liberation from the powers of evil. And third, and most important, the opening of one's life to the liberating power of the Holy Spirit, in trust that God will bring us to himself in his own way. It is in these factors, and not in any morbid or gloomy self-accusation, that Christian penitence consists. As we daily ask God to renew in us a penitent spirit, we are asking him to give us self-knowledge, a realistic apprehension of the consequences of sin (vividly expressed in the picture of Christ crucified), a genuine desire for the rule of love (the Kingdom of God), and the power of the Holy Spirit which assures us that love can and will rule, that even within the wilderness of this world, we are beginning to be transformed into the image of Christ who, having suffered for a while, now reigns in the glory of the Father. Christian penitence is life in the Spirit.

The third main attitude involved in the Christian
life is love. Perhaps no word has been so maligned,
abused, and emptied of meaning as this. But the
central Christian sense of love, *agapē*, has always been
that of concern for another's good and well-being,
whatever one's own emotional feelings about him
may happen to be. Matthew's Gospel (25. 31-46)
relates Jesus' story about how men will be judged on
whether they fed the hungry, showed hospitality to
strangers, helped those ill and in distress, and visited
those in prison. And he goes so far as to say that in
doing these things the Christian is doing them to
Christ; so that every man, however humble, is to be
regarded with the concern and reverence which is
due to the Son of God himself. Luke's parable of the
good Samaritan clearly makes the point that one is
bound to help whomever one encounters who is in
need, whether he is friend or foe; and that this is
what 'loving one's neighbour' consists in. Again,
1 John 4. 19 stresses the point that it is impossible
and absurd to claim to love God if one does not love
one's neighbour.

Thus it is perfectly clear that an essential part of
the Christian life is the service of those in need, whoever they may happen to be; and this extends so far
that one must do even more than is expected of one
(go the second mile; give the coat as well as the
jacket; Matt. 5) in helping one's fellow-men. The person who has the Christian attitude of love is a person
who has the disposition to see his experience in terms
of challenges to personal action, claims upon him to

which he must respond. These demands are the demands which God himself makes upon our lives. He places each of us in a situation in which we can either respond or fail to respond to the demands which are made upon us; and so we develop or fail to develop the ability to love, to respond to the demand of God by acting positively to increase the well-being of others. These demands may be for some action fulfilling an immediate need; or for a more general response of adopting a whole way of life — say, a change of job or interest. In either case, it is part of Christian wisdom to discern what God demands of us in our situation, as the work of love.

Christian love ranges more widely than over human persons, though they are the primary objects of love. One loves by responding to the call of God wherever and whenever it comes; so it is a work of love to conserve the environment, or design a beautiful environment for human living, or ensure that animals are cared for sensibly. Love is the general concern to respond to the call of being to bring higher values into reality, however and wherever it is manifested.

This may give the impression that Christian love is an individual thing, in which an individual responds to some challenge facing him in his own experience. But though it is that, it is also much more. Christian love is an essentially communal thing, a sharing by often very different people of each others' experiences, problems, joys, and struggles. The early Christian word for this is *koinōnia*, a sort of sharing of life with one another. And it is part of the truly Christian experience that the community of Christ is a community of people who are prepared to share each others' lives. This is not the romantic love which lovers have for each other; it is not the love of close friendship which can tie two people together; it is not the companionable love of marriage; it is not the admiring love one has for great figures and heroes. It is *agapē* proper, the concern for another's well-being; but it is *agapē* worked out in the context of a community, in which the members share with each other the interests, purposes, enjoyments, problems, and difficulties involved in putting such love into practice.

It is often said that it is very easy to wish people well when they are far away and out of sight, no personal trouble to oneself. In many ways it is easier to send money for starving people overseas than to deal with the troubles of someone who pesters one from day to day and takes up one's time and energy. Of course, it is very good to send money to good causes. But Christian love demands more than that. It demands one's own personal involvement with people around one. God created us to live with one another, and to discover our own resources by interaction with other people. So Christian love demands that we participate in a community of people who are prepared to share their lives with each other, their troubles and joys.

In such a community, each of us will have his own gifts and talents, and these can be used in the service of the group. Each member should make a definite contribution of something which expresses his distinctive abilities, and which can thus enrich the group. We are all very different people. But each of us, however extrovert or shy, confident or nervous, can add something of value to the life of a group. Of course, that means the group must be extremely careful always to cultivate an atmosphere of goodwill and tolerance. The stronger members must bear up the weaker; each person must be treated with reverence and respect. And the goal should be to aim at the fullest well-being of each member, a well-being which can only be achieved in communal living.

The ideal is often very far from the actual. Many things can go wrong with such a community; it can become cliquish, introverted, or split apart in dissension and acrimony. For these reasons it is probably better for most of us not to aim too high in our common life. Nevertheless, the Christian community only really exists when the members know and meet each other fairly regularly and really take care to listen to the cares and problems of others and think of ways to help. For the Christian, love usually starts in two communities, his family and his church. And it is in those communities that we often realize how costly and difficult love really is; not at all easy do-gooding or superior charity, but hard involvement and the difficult resolution of inevitable conflict with others.

Jesus' love was shown at its highest on the cross; and this shows the real cost of love. To love, we really have to give, to share, to make up our differences and overcome our resentments. And it is important to remember that one capacity which is essential to love is the capacity to accept the love of others as well as to give, and so truly to share. Love is not all giving; it is also the ability to accept gracefully, to allow others to show their love, and to show that it is appreciated. It is helping others to grow in love by pleasing us; and no one has learned love properly who always gives to others but does not accept and encourage their gifts of love to himself. It is because of lack of reciprocity, of sharing and involvement, that do-gooders are sometimes mocked; and

51

our community must above all be one of sharing, so that we can be to one another messengers of reconciliation.

We are called into the church to do this. And the obstacles to love we meet in the church — the people we dislike, the priests who offend us, the services that bore us, the gossip that distracts us — these are the trials which test the real quality and staying-power of our love. In much the same way, the Christian family is a small community in which we are called to love and share together, and develop that peculiar quality of patient love which should mark the Christian life. If love cannot grow in our own family and church, there is not much hope that we can show it in the world at large. Breakdowns occur in both families and churches; and when they do, they must be met with understanding, sympathy, and acceptance by those around. But there can be no doubt that the first place love must grow is in our own homes and churches; and that is where we must all begin.

So love grows first between people who live together, learning to put the good of the others above their own moods and passions and feelings. The gift of peace is that fellowship in the Holy Spirit which God's love brings, when we respond to it. Our own faith-response must be corrected by a sympathetic understanding of others, so that love for the brotherhood characterizes our group.

It is when such love has been established between us, as families and churches, that it must flow out into the world, in service to others in need. The church is called to be the body of Christ, incarnating the love of Christ in the world now just as Jesus did long ago in Palestine. St Theresa said: 'Christ has no body now on earth but yours, no hands but yours, no

52

feet but yours. Yours are the eyes through which Christ's compassion is to look out on the world. Yours are the feet with which he is to go about doing good. Yours are the hands with which he is to bless men now.' It is for us to repeat the miracles of healing and service and forgiveness which were shown dramatically in the life of Jesus. We are to give food to those in need, hospitality to those who ask, and comfort to those in distress. We are to care dispassionately for the well-being of others. As Plato wrote in the *Republic*, a good man cannot ever bring himself to harm anyone, however evil; and that is surely the authentic message of the Lord who died a criminal's death rather than deal violently with the forces which opposed him.

LORD, forgive me

for my failure to appreciate the beauty I have seen,
for my timidity and laziness in creative action,
for my failure to consider the good of the people
I have met and to help them constructively and
positively,
for the lack of sensitivity which has led me to
offend or harm others,
for lack of judgement in coming to decisions,
for failure to consider all the facts or weigh up all
the arguments,
for the times I have closed my mind to things I do
not want to know and have caricatured opinions I do
not share;
forgive me for the idle words which hurt, the half-
truths which distort, the insincerities which betray
my own self-centredness,
for my lack of joy, my obsessive concern with my
own problems,
for the difficulty I have in giving way to sponta-
neous enthusiasm, in recovering the infectious laugh-
ter of children, being happy in simple things,
for dwelling on the past with nostalgia and regret
and on the future with foreboding and anxiety,
for not cherishing the present moment in simpli-
city.

Enliven my mind, that I may see and respond to
the claims which are made upon me today.
help me not to be afraid of other people, not to
think of myself and the impression I make, but to
share, to give and to accept love;
help me to remember that other people have
problems and difficulties which I may hardly guess
at;

help me to care for them without expecting gratitude;

help me to allow others to show their love;

help me to love those who bore, offend, or oppose me;

help me to accept people as they are, and not to be always trying to mould them the way I want them to be.

Lord, you have made us to do your will;
   deliver us from ignorance and desire,
   and set us free to show your love.

8 PATIENCE

The character of Christian love is beautifully portrayed in 1 Cor. 13, a deservedly well-loved passage from the New Testament letters. It is worth considering this passage in depth and making it a frequent subject of meditation. For the sort of loving personality sketched in that short paragraph is the epitome of what the fulfilled Christian life should be. To seek to think of these qualities and incorporate them ever more fully into one's own life is to explore Christian love in a practical and transforming way.

The passage runs as follows: 'Love is patient; love is kind and envies no one. Love is never boastful nor conceited nor rude; never selfish, nor quick to take offence. Love keeps no score of wrongs; does not gloat over other men's sins, but delights in the truth. There is nothing love cannot face; there is no limit to its faith, its hope and its endurance.'

(1) Love is patient, is prepared to wait, not to force the issue, not to push things through the way one wants to see them, but, having striven for good, to leave the outcome in the hand of God. It is not perturbed by things that go wrong and by obstacles on the way. It sets its eyes on a goal and works slowly but relentlessly towards that goal. Patience and endurance go together; for patient love is tenacious and undeterred by obstacles. And it can be patient because it is rooted in faith, the confidence that all creatures will be brought to their final good at last, by God's power; and the knowledge that one is only an instrument in God's hands and must leave the

outcome of one's acts to him. Love requires endless patience, for often we cannot see the effect our acts have, or they seem to have no effects. But we must not give way to impatience or anger, for the effects will come in God's way and in God's time. One of the outstanding examples of the patience of faith is found in Charles de Foucauld, who felt called by God to the desert life and prayed for others to join him. No one came, and he was eventually killed, his prayers evidently unanswered. Yet his patience was rewarded, quite unknown to him; for thirty years after his death the influence of his life led to a great movement of spiritual reform throughout large areas of the Christian church; his prayers, formed in patience, were answered. Love must never give up and never try to force the issue.

(2) Love is kind. It is not cruel, hurting people's feelings or being inconsiderate towards them. And it is not over-protective, sapping personal initiative and independence. It treats men gently and is not flustered by antagonistic reactions. Cruelty and inconsiderateness are very evident in our world; and ironically, one of the most common ways of being cruel is by sticking rigidly to rules of morality or propriety, even when faced with a person in need. The cruelties 'moral' people can show to those who have transgressed moral rules are enormous. One must always take care to remember that kindness is itself a major moral virtue, so that to lack it is undoubtedly to be immoral oneself. To be kind is to ensure that people feel that they can find encouragement and support rather than condemnation and exclusion; to put people at ease and offer them the possibility of a real human relationship. It is the very opposite of being

patronizing; it is the preparedness to open up personal relationships in a way which transforms and humanizes the rather impersonal application of moral standards. This in no sense undermines real and worthwhile moral standards; on the contrary, it emphasizes their real basis in care for the happiness and integrity of all human persons. Kindness is the essential humanizing element in the practice of morality.

(3) Love does not envy; it does not look at the health or life or possessions of others and regret that they have these good things. That is because Christians know we possess the best and most lasting promise of all, the promise of eternal life with God. It is not for us to wish for lives we have not been granted by God, to wish we were someone or somewhere else. Envy is the wish to possess what another person possesses, even though that is not possible; so it involves a dissatisfaction with our own lives, by comparison with others. It is difficult not to envy in this world, where goods are distributed unjustly and disproportionately. Yet we are called to remember that love must be shown in a loveless world by a certain measure of self-sacrifice. We may certainly try to get the things we want; we may even wish we had good things we do not have; but we must not become discontented because other people's lives seem better than our own.

(4) Love does not boast; for we know all we have is ultimately a gift from God, even when our own efforts have helped to use these gifts. There are inequalities in the world; but we must neither desire what belongs to others nor boast about what we have. To boast is to seek to gain a psychological advantage

over others by stressing that we are in a relatively better position. It may be true that we have advantages which some others lack; but to use these to gain some psychological advantage in fact demonstrates our own essential feeling of insecurity. In love, we should be able to approach others openly, not wishing to impress or over-awe, but rather to discover and enjoy what is of mutual interest or concern. The truly loving, psychologically secure person is one who does not need to seek to impress, for he is able to offer himself and his own interests as he is and to learn from the different experience of the people with whom he meets.

(5) We must not be proud or conceited, thinking ourselves better than others. Neither should we be unduly self-deprecatory, thinking that we are much worse than others, or totally useless. Love requires that we make a realistic assessment of the sorts of things we are good at, but that we then regard these things as gifts to be used in the service of others. It is only natural to feel pride at times in one's achievements; but one must not bask in others' admiration for its own sake, and one should try to ensure that one really serves others. Admiration can be a dangerous thing, for sometimes we have to do things that will cause others to cease to admire us, and we must be ready to do so if necessary. It is not pride in achievement which love rules out; it is that form of conceit which seeks and delights in the admiration of others, as something sought for its own sake. Clearly, the world does contain the possibility of seeking admiration for its own sake; and this desire for status is one of the things which lead men to oppress their fellows and exact tribute from them. So injustice

arises, as the exercise of partiality and the refusal to regard the claims of others as on a par with one's own. Love must seek justice, as the dispassionate treatment of all men, with a concern for the ultimate good of every individual, without partiality or exception.

(6) Love is not rude. It does not try to make other people look silly or feel uncomfortable. We are often unintentionally rude, by just not realizing the feelings of the other person and taking time to make him feel at ease. Etiquette, good manners, is a virtue of love in that it always tries to put others at ease. It goes very wrong when it becomes embodied in a set of exclusive social rules, by which one set of people can be distinguished from others (the 'peasants'). No loving community will ever be such that visitors, whoever they are, feel excluded, disregarded, or looked down on. Love accepts and treats all people with respect and consideration. There is a lesson here for many of our churches, which can sometimes become exclusive social clubs or even spiritual cliques. That is just rude; and it undermines love. One only has to read the correspondence columns of a church magazine to realize how rude many Christians are. They often seem to take a delight in denigrating and misunderstanding their opponents. They quickly become angry and are quick to condemn. Rudeness, lack of consideration for fully understanding the views of others, seems to come very naturally to people who think they have the full truth, that there is nothing to learn from others. Even though love is one of the chief virtues of religion, it can be difficult to be part of a religious group and love; for, human nature being what it is, we quickly come to stand for certain views

or beliefs, and quickly become rude to those who disagree with us. Rudeness leads to intolerance and that narrow-mindedness which cannot learn from others; it leads to the erection of rules which exclude others from consideration; in the end, it leads to fear of those one opposes, and to hatred; and at that point, the worship of God ceases to exist and becomes demonic. Where there is no love, sympathy, and understanding, the worship of God becomes not only worthless but positively harmful.

(7) Love is not selfish. It considers the needs and desires of others and does not simply take what it wants, first. That does not mean that one must always give up what one wants. Nothing is more irritating than the person who says, 'No, you have it; I will do without.' One does have the same rights as the next man, not less. All that is required is that one does not make one's own claim more important than his. One must try to consider one's own case as though one was a quite disinterested judge. So love tries to ensure that others are treated equitably.

(8) Love is not quick to take offence. Others often do or say things which hurt us, annoy us, or irritate us; it is very often our pride which is hurt on these occasions. We must try not to react by being rude or angry in return; and the best thing to do is to tell the person concerned honestly what has offended us. That may not end the matter; and if it is a dangerous slander, one may need to take steps to counteract it. Nevertheless, one must always attempt to forgive others, to be prepared to talk to and mix with them; and, while perhaps not being able to like them, always to seek their good whenever possible and never to seek to cause them harm out of a feeling of revenge. This is a very hard saying; when personal relations break down, it is very tempting to retaliate by causing harm to others through gossip or in some other way. If we continue to desire their good, even when taking action to alleviate the evil consequences of their acts, perhaps, we rarely have the satisfaction

of admiration and respect. We are more liable to get misunderstanding and incomprehension. Here again, one must not look for immediate consequences of one's attitude; but one cannot tell what long-term consequences may have been begun by loving instead of retaliating. So we must not take offence or give offence to any man, though it is allowable to take steps to disprove a slander.

(9) Love does not count up wrongs, either of oneself or others. It does not store them up and hold them against people. Resentment destroys love and arises through thinking of the bad things others have done to one. Another common human tendency is to judge others without a sympathetic understanding of their circumstances and point of view. As long as others persist in evil, one cannot condone their conduct; and, if it affects others, one cannot allow it to go unchecked. Even then, one should be primarily concerned to understand why the other person acts as he does, what may have made him like that; and to help him see the consequences of his behaviour and turn from them. We should, in other words, always be ready to help, whenever our help may be asked for, rather than to condemn. Condemnation helps no one; and it may destroy our characters by building up anger and resentment. Love will always look for the positive goods to be developed in others and will not concentrate on their bad points, keeping score of all the bad and silly things they do. One of the secrets of good human relationships is to look for and stress the good points others have; and, if one must keep score, to keep score of those.

(10) Love does not gloat over the failures of others, physical, financial, or moral. It is so easy to be

63

secretly pleased when someone's plans come to nothing or when they show themselves to be less than perfect. Whenever a public figure is found out in some weakness or vice, thousands of people leap with glee to condemn and vilify, even though they can know little of the circumstances; for they are (secretly) pleased to see the mighty fall. It is important to see that all human beings, however great, have their failings. But these failures are not things to be pleased about. Whenever such a feeling arises, we should remember our own frailty and consider how we can help to make such failures more palatable.

(11) Love delights in the truth. It does not indulge in lies or hearsay gossip or half-truths. It is not satisfied with glib generalizations or hasty conclusions drawn from insufficient evidence. It seeks to know what is true and limit itself to claiming knowledge where it is justified. Very much damage is done in human affairs by leaping to conclusions about other people or by retailing a story which is not really known to be true, but which is juicy gossip. To be concerned for truth is to be concerned really to understand how other people see things. It is not to put one's own position in the best light and treat one's opponents' views as absurd or distorted. It has been true even in the history of the church that theologians have distorted the views of others by not bothering to understand them properly. A good example of this is the incredible way in which some Christian preachers have treated Judaism as simply a legalistic and hard-hearted faith, without any real spiritual life at all. That is a gross perversion of the facts, which could only be achieved by ignoring most of the spiritual writings of Judaism and reading only the more obviously extreme and

bizarre forms of Jewish thought. In our world, it is more and more important to cease pigeon-holing people and making massive condemnations of views we do not know about or have no sympathy with. It is just not good enough to condemn Marxism outright, without ever having read the larger part of Marx's writings, just on the basis of a few polemical, unsympathetic, and possibly ignorant remarks one has heard from some parent or teacher. The truth is the hardest of all things to discover, and there is no easy way to discover it. A precondition of finding it is sympathy and understanding. And so it is that even in intellectual and religious debate − or especially then, perhaps − love is required to discover the truth and see things from others' points of view, rather than as distorted by one's own ignorant prejudices.

(12) Love can face anything. Suffering, injury, opposition, death, deprivation − all these things can be met with love, the determined disposition to care for the good of persons. Whatever happens to us, nothing can take from us the will to love; and in that sense, as Plato said, the good man can never be harmed; for our highest good is found in responding to the challenge of personal disaster by submitting to God and transforming the potentially destructive power of evil into good, by meeting it without resentment, depression, and irritability; but with gratitude for the hope of life to come, acceptance and joy in the presence of the Creator. Love is the response to the challenge of being; and as we come to see this challenge more clearly, we thereby come to apprehend the Holy One who calls us to our own final good, the one who claims our lives absolutely. Even when, through pain and disability, we can take no

other positive action, it is always open to us to respond by obedience to his will and trust in his hope. Love involves limitless faith, the turning to God who can sustain us in his love. He gives us the delight of his presence, and he fills our lives with his love, enabling us to love others, to be really concerned about and interested in them. Love involves limitless hope that all things will be brought to their final good and that we must help in this process insofar as we can. Love involves unlimited endurance, in that whatever evils beset us, we can go on in the strength that God gives, knowing that he calls us to himself above all things.

So the nature of Christian love is clearly set out, to be shown both in intimate personal relationships within our own community and in helping those in need more generally. What basically underlies this attitude is that one must respect all persons for their unique, unrepeatable value, created by God for an eternal destiny; one must share sympathetically with all men in their needs and troubles, as Christ shared and suffered with and for us; and one must be involved with others in an exploration of that mutual personal relationship which the doctrine of the Trinity suggests as a faint reflection of the interior life of God himself. These sorts of love do not exhaust the Christian life — for that one has to speak of the love of God himself — but they represent the natural outflowing response of man to the forgiving and renewing vision and power of God, and an essential and indispensable part of the Christian way in the world.

LORD, we pray for the patience of love; that does not look for immediate results or become deterred by obstacles and difficulties;

we pray for the kindness of love; that we may learn to be gentle and considerate, to put people at their ease, and to meet others with understanding and tolerance;

we pray for the contentment of love; which does not envy what others have or resent their good fortune, which remains firm through all outward changes of fortune;

we pray for the humility of love; that we may seek not to impress others, but come to an honest estimate of ourselves; that we may not depend too much on the admiration of others, but be ready to face hostility for the cause of right;

we pray for the wisdom of love, that we may be sensitive to the feelings and interests of others, and treat all people with respect and consideration; that we may look for the good in people, be ready to forgive and slow to condemn; that we may seek to understand and to learn from others, and to share their joys and sorrows; that we may judge wisely and with discernment;

we pray for the passionate concern of love; that we may not put ourselves and our own interests first, but consider impartially the good of all, and actively pursue justice and equity for all men;

we pray for the equanimity of love; that we may not take offence at the actions of others, and may not give offence by anger, irritation, or thoughtlessness;

we pray for the compassion of love; that we may not judge others harshly, or harbour resentment against them; that we may grieve over their failures, and help them achieve their purposes;

we pray for the honesty of love; that we may refrain from gossip and half-truth, from hasty judgement and from assertions made in ignorance; we pray for a positive concern for the truth, for an adequate understanding of others and for a delight in the discovery of truth;

we pray for the fidelity of love; that we may be faithful to ourselves, to each other, and to you; that, founding our lives on your faithfulness, we may stand firm and unshakeable in your unconquerable love;

we pray for the assurance of love; that we may know that all things may be turned to good; that, in all that we undergo, God's love which made us to be will call us to final fulfilment; so give us hope, that we may remember the goal which is set before us, and not lose heart;

we pray for the endurance of love; that we may have the strength to meet suffering, opposition, deprivation, and death with the unchanging will to love.

Lord Jesus Christ, you gave your life in love for men; grant us a share in your passion for the world, that we and all men may be transfigured into your glory.

Christian love is essentially a response to the love of God and a channelling of God's love into the world through man. So it depends upon the faith that God's love will inspire and sustain us, that he will bring all things to a final consummation, and that love can overcome any evil. But the Christian view that the universe is governed by and directed towards love must meet the very great difficulty occasioned by the existence of suffering and evil in the world. Looking at disease, war, famine, and violent death, one may well be driven to ask, how can such an evil world be made by love? Although this difficulty is very real, and the experience of evil prevents many from coming to Christian belief, I think that one can gain some idea of how this world, with all its imperfections, may be shaped by love. Not only can the fact of evil not be shown to contradict the existence of a loving God; but an appreciation of the sort of love shown on the cross may disclose in a more positive way how this world can forward a purpose of ultimate love.

If one thinks for a moment of the nature of God as it has been construed in the Christian tradition, one gains an idea of what may be called God's internal love. As a Trinity of Father, Son, and Holy Spirit, the being of God exemplifies a love which is creative, issuing in new experiments and adventures as the expression of infinite creative power; mutually shared, a social rather than an individual reality; and beatific — that is, perfectly without defect, but completely fulfilled and supremely happy. These characteristics can be said to define the being of God, which John speaks of as *being* love. God does not just possess the property of being loving; his Trinitarian nature as creative, social, and beatific is the nature of supreme love itself. To enter heaven is to share in that love; to enter hell is to exclude oneself from it. God will never give up desiring and working for the final good of all his creatures; but men have the freedom to reject even that unchanging love, and so to enter the state conceived in New Testament imagery as a rubbish-heap, a world of shades or outer darkness. But though man may enter into God's love, it is important to see that this love differs from the sort of love that men can have here in this world. The sort of love outlined in 1 Cor. 13 – patient, kind, enduring, humble love – is a sort of love which carries with it the possibility of defect, of falling and failing, of trial and error and slow struggle towards an ideal goal. Human love involves suffering, struggle, and freedom; and those things are part of what makes human love possible.

The implications of this truth are immense. It means that in human existence it is possible to realize values which are not to be found in the being of God himself. They are not to be found there for the very reason that his love is changeless, eternal, and perfect, and therefore cannot be the sort of struggling love we come to know when God tears us apart to recreate us into fuller being. There is a supreme value in human love, the love of a creature which is free to accept or reject the gifts and demands of the Creator; which has to struggle to achieve what is required of it; which evolves from a condition of alienation, by responding to the dim challenge which calls it back to its source. God is not free to be either loving or hateful; he does not have to struggle to find himself; he cannot be alienated from himself without ceasing to be God. Thus by the creation of man specific and distinctive values are brought into being which could not otherwise have existed. When God created man, he created beings with the ability to respond to him; but that implies the ability to keep one's being and refuse to respond. So, by creating this world with all its risks, God chose to bring into being new values which can only exist in the sort of world we know.

To take just one central example; if there is any virtue in the attitude of patient love, it seems that the world must be such as to contain obstacles and difficulties. There must exist temptations to be impatient or indolent, which are the two main ways in which patience can fail. That is, we must be able to take things into our own hands and override other people or push for what we want at their expense. Or we must be able to sit back and do nothing and thereby lose the opportunity of doing things that should be done. That these possibilities should exist is necessary to the existence of love as we conceive it. Our world is full of people who have fallen into these temptations; who are trying to get their own way, push their own view of things, force things to come out as they want, against all opposition. And it is also full of people who apathetically watch the world go by and do not bring about the good things which they could bring about. Thus many good things never come into being, and many things come into being which cause conflict and disruption; and the patient love which always strives for good but leaves the outcome in God's hands is continually opposed both by indifference and by human ambition and inflexibility. In such a world, physical needs and mental sorrows inevitably come about as men are either indifferent to each other or trample on each other's desires in the pursuit of their own aims. And so, in our world, love comes to take the form we know, of a difficult and costly rescue-operation, trying to show men whose lives have been blighted by indifference and callousness the higher way of patient love, which consists in caring for the well-being of others in a positive, active way, but never trying to force its own solutions on other people, never giving up when not reciprocated, always content to leave the effects to work secretly on others, without looking for immediate results, gratitude, or return of any apparent sort.

The Kingdom of Heaven is the fulfilment of love, a society of perpetual love. There no suffering or physical need exists; yet patient love can still exist, as a concern for others, an interest in their lives, and a sharing of interests and enjoyments. Perhaps, too, there will be possibilities of helping others to attain their purposes, and we will be able to co-operate in finding new ways to be creative and express the glory of created being. Such a perfect love, in which all men could creatively co-operate in the attainment of joint purposes, is far beyond present human attainment. And it may well be that its attainment must be learned in the difficult conditions of a world wherein lack of love is a possibility and a temptation for all of us, and where we must then cope with the complexities caused by the actions of those who do lack love. This world can be seen, then, as a training-ground for love; and though it may not be inevitable that suffering and sorrow come into such a world, their possibility is implied in the very nature of love; so the fact that they exist, though it is tragic, is scarcely surprising to those who see what love means.

God's promise of salvation is that all men can

attain perfect love and that they will do so by being filled with the love of God himself, as they open their lives to him in faith. It is the function of the church to proclaim and foreshadow that fulfilment. The church is not the ship of the elect sailing safely to salvation, leaving millions to die in despair and agony. The church is the community of those called by God to declare the light in the midst of darkness and try to live by it, and to call others to that light. The church always needs to point beyond itself; for the church, too, is an ambiguous, worldly phenomenon, and love is not always its most obvious sign. So the church points always to the Lord of the church, the risen Christ who offers his presence and love to be lived out in the lives of those who come to him. But Christ should be found in the church; and he will be, as the church learns to rely on his strength alone.

Membership of the church is primarily a responsibility, a calling to be the light of the world, the beginnings of that perfect fellowship of love for which we hope in heaven. We should not ask what the church can offer us. We should ask what God calls us to do within the community of the church. For membership is not our choice; it is God's calling. And what the church primarily proclaims is not a set of intellectual beliefs, but a fellowship of love which is the pattern of a perfect society dimly foreshadowed in its life. It is, of course, morally much easier to see the church's proclamation solely in terms of clearly defined beliefs — the virgin birth, the miracles, the resurrection — we can assent to such things without any moral effort, and perhaps with merely a twinge of intellectual doubt on occasion. It is much more difficult, and much more challenging, to see the church's proclamation as being to set the pattern of love for the world, to see it in terms of renewed lives and committed service. Of course it is more difficult. But let there be no doubt; at the end of our life we will be judged on love, and if the church does not or cannot say, 'Here God calls you to a life centred on love, an exploration together of what love means in a world like this', if it does not say that first, the church will not be worth preserving, however orthodox its creeds.

LORD, you have called us into the community of the
church that we may show light in the darkness of
the world and foreshadow in ourselves the pattern
of your rule of love;
help us to point beyond ourselves to you, to live by
grace and in your power,
to let your love be shown in our lives, that our
acts and words may manifest your forgiving, healing,
and reconciling love.

We ask that, as we turn to you, your love may
dwell in us so that, in loving you, our love becomes
one with your love manifest in us,
and we are exalted by your grace to share in
your eternal life, and serve mankind in your name
and your power.

Lord, fill our hearts with the radiance of your resurrection, that we may be delivered from the darkness
of death into eternal light.

The Christian life is founded on an ultimate optimism, an ultimate hope; for Christians believe that the whole world is in process of redemption. The resurrection of Jesus is a foreshadowing of the new fulfilment which is to come to all creation, as it is reconciled to God. Although the New Testament writers had no idea of evolution as they wrote, yet that idea is a very natural expression of the Christian vision of human life as 'fallen' into the world or alienated from God; and as being reconciled to God through a slow and often painful learning of love, patience, and peace. 'The whole created universe groans in all its parts as if in the pangs of childbirth' (Rom. 8. 22); and 'The sufferings we now endure bear no comparison with the splendour, as yet unrevealed, which is in store for us. For the created universe waits with eager expection for God's sons to be revealed' (Rom. 8. 19-20). Here is the picture of creation anxiously waiting for the revelation of the new creation, men born of God's Spirit.

What the first Christians expected was a sudden, longed-for end to the present world order, a revelation of Christ in glory and redemption of human life from pain, slavery, and inadequacy, and the removal of every imperfection. We have a quite different picture of the universe — the picture of earth as one tiny planet among millions of stars, with millions of years still before us, and no sudden close-down of history to be expected. Our hope is not for the imminent return of Christ in glory, coming in the clouds with hosts of angels. Yet there are two important things which this early Christian imagery has to say to us. One is that human history has a point and a purpose; the world is not just 'one damn thing after another', nor is it something to be escaped from. The purpose of history is to bring into being the Kingdom of God, in which men can love freely and fully. How that will happen, we do not know; but we have our part to play in the new creation; we are 'fellow-workers with God' in bringing about his Kingdom. Christian hope is a hope for this world, and it sees our present acts and sufferings as having a part to play in the transfiguration of this world.

The second point is that what we await is the *parousia*, the being-present, the making-manifest, of Christ. It is not a matter of relying on human effort, of bringing the Kingdom into being by sheer moral effort and will-power. It is a matter of being eagerly on the lookout for the coming of Christ in human lives. Again and again the New Testament writers speak of 'keeping alert', of 'being awake', of 'being watchful and expectant'. Each day we must be filled with the eager anticipation that Christ will come, even when we least expect him. He will come in the face of the poor man who asks for bread or a drink (Matt. 25. 31-40). He will come in the song of a bird or the delicate shape of a flower. He will come in sadness and pain, consoling and refreshing with a strong, gentle power. He will come into our common life, making reconciliation and renewal possible. He will come at the moment of death, a moment not within our power, to take us to himself. He will come in glory at the end of time, the consummation of all things, when all creation is bound to God for eternity. But at all times we must be looking for his approach, enabling him to make himself known, to

77

give us himself. And at all times we must be looking beyond all times, to the consummation and uniting of all things in Christ, when 'the universe, all in heaven and on earth, might be brought into a unity in Christ' (Eph. 1. 10). We look, then, to 'the wealth and glory of the share he offers . . . among his people in their heritage' (Eph. 1. 19). We look for a fellowship with all those who have died, when all are united in God, sharing the vision of God in the community of his people. As Paul writes in Corinthians, the life we shall live is as different from and more glorious than this as the flower is from the seed which died to give it life. The Christian hope is that Christ will come as we watch daily for him, to give us now through his Spirit an intimation of the immortality which we will have in his love.

If we have this hope then it is possible to accept tragedy and pain as inextricably bound up with the sort of life we have, and to accept all things from the hand of God, even at times of desolation and anguish. For, after all, we could only exist as the people we are in a world very like this, with all its sorrows and losses. We may think it would have been better for God to create a perfect world, full of perfect people. But if he had, we certainly wouldn't be part of it. With all our faults, hopes, despairs, pains, and joys, we are part and parcel of this world, where nature operates in accordance with stable and general laws, where life evolves through a process of creative conflict and advance, and where the ambiguities and complexities of life add a poignancy and depth to existence which could hardly otherwise exist. We do not have to think that this is the best of all possible worlds. If we think of our lives as worth having, especially in view of the hope Jesus offers us, then we are prepared to say that this universe was worth creating, that it is good.

It is part of the Christian hope that every sentient creature will find an appropriate fulfilment after death. The nature of our present sufferings will contribute to the unique character of our final joy. We are told that Christ endured the shame and suffering of the cross for the sake of the glory that was set before him, and that all the sufferings of this present time do not compare with the joy that lies ahead of us. So the hope of eternal life places our present brief lives in a wider and more acceptable context. Moreover, the relation of present suffering and future joy is not just an accidental, external one. The nature of our present sufferings will be so transformed that we will have a sort of joy that could only have come through and out of the sufferings which were uniquely our own. Our future destiny will be seen and known to have a special sort of fulfilment that could only have come out of sufferings such as ours.

In creating this world, God foresaw the possibility of pain, sin, suffering, and death. He foresaw the cross and his participation in the pain of creation. But he also foresaw that the sort of good which could come out of such a world was a distinctive sort of good worth creating, which could not otherwise have existed. There is perhaps a value which we cannot fully understand in the life of moral struggle and challenge which we now live, in the freedom of creatures both to disobey their moral calling and to be distanced from a too obvious, omnipresent providence of God. Maybe our painful independence of God and our ability to strive and respond to the challenge of God's will in a distorted universe and to share in the creative striving of God as a co-creator of the world's future, have a value which we can now only dimly appreciate.

The Christian believes, too, that God does not merely watch our sufferings from afar; he shares in suffering, even in creating the world. As William Temple put it, there is a cross in the heart of God at the beginning of creation. In some way we cannot understand, the creation of free rational beings such as we are involves the suffering of God himself, bringing life from death and sorrow, transforming the nature of man as, by legend, the wood of the cross pierced the skull of Adam and became the tree of life, bringing joy to the world.

Perhaps the most appropriate parable of the human situation, as the Christian sees it, is to be found in the story of the Prodigal Son (Luke 15. 12-24). In this world, we are in the position of sons who squander their inheritance in a distant country. The exploration of the possibilities of our world may lead to disillusionment, suffering, and disaster; but it is somehow our destiny to live out of our own resources, in exile from God, until we come to our senses and seek to return to our true home. Then we shall find that God's love for us is as unchanging as ever, and our homecoming, the end of our self-imposed journeyings, will be the place where we began. We live now in a far country; but our final destiny is to return to the one who even now shares in our sufferings and calls us to himself. For God is not only conceived as the changeless eternal love of the Father; he is also the suffering Christ on the cross and the creative Spirit striving and groaning within men to bring to birth a world of righteousness and real love. If the Christian way in this world is in a sense an exile, it is also a sharing in the passion of Christ to create out of a world of freedom and loss the new kingdom of love and peace into which he calls us. Evil and suffering is a permanent possibility of human life in this world; but from the cross of suffering, love grows in glory until it transfigures the whole creation. It is the Christian calling to share in the passion of Christ, that we and all our world may be transfigured into his glory.

COME, LORD, and show yourself to us today,
   in the face of the poor man who asks for a meal,
   in the faces of the oppressed who cry out for
   justice,
   in the faces of the sick who ask for healing.

Come, Lord, into our hearts, refreshing us when we are tired, renewing our vision and restoring our strength.

Come, Lord, among us, breaking the barriers that divide us.

Come, Lord, at the hour of our death, when light and dark are made clear, and take us to yourself.

Come, Lord, at the end of time, when all things are taken up into God, and show to us the fulness of the glory of God.

Come, Lord, and give us now a share in your eternity, that, as we walk in the way of your cross, you may lead us in the path of resurrection.

The Christian believes that it is part of his concern for the world to pray for it. Of course, Christians should work for the good of others in material ways; and if they do not, their prayers are not liable to be much use. But intercessory prayer is an important aspect of Christian love. Intercession is not just a sort of auto-suggestion, so that if we pray about others we come to do more for them ourselves and may manage to screw our courage and concern up a little. Neither is it some automatic process of putting in requests to a cosmic computer which then decides to say yes to some, no to others, and ignore others completely. It is essential to see intercession as a part of the general raising of the heart and mind to God. It is thinking of the needs and concerns of others and bringing those needs before God in thought. We may indeed pray for specific things — for example, for someone who is ill to recover. But that is really a recognition of how we see that their obvious need can best be met; and while it is proper for us to pray for their needs to be met, we must allow that we cannot always see the best way of meeting them, in the long term; nor can we know the incredibly complex way in which their lives must be inextricably interwoven with the lives of others.

So we think of the needs of others — the church, our country, our friends, our enemies, and all who are sick in mind or body. Thinking of them, we raise the mind to adore and love God and simply place those needs before him. One of the best ways of doing this is just to picture the person concerned in one's mind

and ask God to meet his need. We do not have to
spend a long time or to feel very intensely about
these intercessions. Sometimes we may be filled with
deep emotion about some subject and may spend a
long time in prayer. But most often it is enough just
to mention the need and ask for it to be met, in the
general context of our worship.

We should seek first to see what the true needs are;
second, to ask that they be met; and third, to see if
and how we may help to meet them ourselves. It may
be a good idea to commit oneself to a certain time of
prayer and quiet — say, fifteen minutes — for a
specific subject. In that time one may do many
things: just keep silence, waiting for God to speak if
he will; or say some set prayers, psalms, or devotions.
All that is necessary is to keep the time with the intention of offering it for the need one has in mind. It
is not necessary to keep that need explicitly in mind
all the time; just let it come and go as it naturally
does.

What will this accomplish? Our Lord clearly taught
that prayer, especially if it is made in a group of people meeting together with a common mind, does have
a point and effect. It is a power, freely contributed
by us, which God uses to effect his purposes in the
world. Just as we can help one another in physical
ways, or refuse to do so, so we can help one another
by prayer, or refuse to do so. To ask why God should
have given us this power is really to ask why he made
a world in which people are left alone to help one
another and to depend upon one another to a great
extent. We cannot answer this question; but it is entirely consistent with the nature of the world we
know, in which others in need do depend upon our
help, that asking for the needs of others to be met in

prayer should be itself a means of helping them.

Naturally, the situation is extremely complex. People are free agents and cannot be forced to do things against their will. People may have all sorts of mixed motives in their prayers, or they may see the needs of others wrongly or not see how they should be met for the greatest ultimate good. So it is not possible to set up experimental conditions for prayer, to test the probability of satisfactory answers. All one can say is that one's prayers will be among those factors contributing to the outcome of human situations and will influence them for good. It is useless to try to probe the mind of God and see how he might decide to answer our prayers. We can be sure that all our prayers will be answered, in that they will be accepted by God and used for good. But we can never be sure how, and we can never determine why some prayers are answered directly and in a spectacular way, while others appear to go completely unheard — that is, they are not used at all in the way we intended or wished. Yet we may believe that all true prayer for the needs of others contributes to a sort of spiritual reservoir of good will, which is a positive force for good in a world so much beset by strong powers of evil and malice.

We should not think of God waiting for requests and then deciding what to do. Rather, we should think of God's general providential care for the universe, working in many ways to bring all together for good, and using the various plans and intentions of men to draw all together into one vast complex design. Our prayers are among the factors which he uses in guiding the overall scheme of things, parts of our co-operation with his loving purposes. Such prayers can release a power that seems to affect the course of events in strange, unpredictable, but somehow 'ordered' ways. As William Temple put it beautifully, 'When I pray, co-incidences begin to happen.'

It is not only our mental or vocal prayers which God uses in this way. Our whole lives, and especially our own sufferings, can be properly speaking prayers offered to God for the needs of others. We are healed by the offering of the life of Jesus; and our lives, too, can become prayers of sacrifice, offered for the needs of the world. In vocal and explicit intercessions we simply make articulate and precise our self-offering, the 'true and living sacrifice' of a life dedicated to God. In the providence of God our self-sacrifice is taken up and used for the healing of the world, as it expresses a conformity of our will to the mind and will of God himself. Our sacrifice is never an automatic obtaining of power; it is an offering to God, which may be used in ways inconceivable by us to increase the power of good in the world. By the offering of the Eucharist, of daily liturgical prayer, and of lives of service and obedience to God's will, we can be channels of love, mediators who offer the needs of men to God, by whose prayers the world is consecrated to God and his kingdom of righteousness and peace brought nearer. It is one of the great responsibilities of the Christian calling to live vicariously for all men, and by our dedication to bring others nearer to God, the source and goal of their lives.

Intercession, then, is the continual disposition to offer up our own lives in obedience to God's will, on behalf of the needs of ourselves and of all men. Augustine puts this point very well in writing of the Eucharist as a sacrifice in which the offering is the people themselves and their daily lives: 'The city of the redeemed itself, the congregation and society of the saints, is offered as an universal sacrifice to God by the High-Priest . . . this is the sacrifice of Christians . . . The church celebrates it in the sacrament of the altar . . . in which it is shown that in what she offers, she herself is offered' (*De Civitate Dei*, 10. 6). In the Eucharist we are created as a people holy to God and offered to him in union with Christ; and this conception of our lives as a sacrifice offered in union with that of Christ plays a central part in the Christian life.

Explicit prayers for others express a focusing of the mind on particular issues; but the whole of the Christian life should be a perpetual sacrifice, offered up in intercession for all men. This reflects the truth that 'no man is an island'; but the destiny of each is closely and inevitably bound up with the destinies of all. When Christians talk of the 'communion of saints', they have in mind this close interrelation of all men to one another. Humanity is bound together for better or worse, and as we pray for others, so others continue to pray for us; and all mankind, living and dead, is thus tied together in mutual concern, which is a foretaste of that perfect unity in the love of God for which we hope; the vision of God in the community of all God's people. We achieve true intercession when our lives are so transformed by Christ that he lives out in us his sacrificial life, offered for all men; and we become simply the means through which he continues to offer up his eternal sacrifice for the needs of the world. True intercession is a life lived for others and offered to God, through the power of Christ whose love recreates and unites us together in himself.

13 COMMITMENT

The Christian life is the life of a person who tries at all times and situations in his life to cultivate the dispositions of reverence, penitence, and love. Such a person will attempt to reverence and delight in all that is of value; feel gratitude for all that is good; examine himself, acknowledge his failures and inadequate responses, and turn to rely on God's power; be concerned to bring all creation to its proper fulfilment and try to love those he encounters. This complex of attitudes, by constant interplay and interaction upon each other, gradually builds up a basic and enduring character which is able to respond creatively to all things, which brings happiness, creativity, and love, which is able even to accept pain and sorrow as a sharing in the passion of the love of Christ, and which looks to a future consummation in glory of what is partially seen and achieved in this life.

Christian faith is first and foremost a practical thing, a way of feeling, willing, and acting. It makes all the difference to one's life, because it transforms the quality of all day-to-day activities. The Christian way is a discipline leading to human fulfilment (salvation), a discipline of prayer, meditation, and love in action, a discipline whose aim is to change the human mind and heart radically and completely. And the starting point for Christian faith is the practical commitment it asks for. I become a Christian by entering into the Christian way of life; and if I have reverence and penitence and love in their fulness, then I am on the way to being conformed to the image of Christ; I am a Christian.

But the Christian life is not just the cultivation of certain attitudes by a self-imposed discipline. These attitudes, and the commitment to the discipline, arise out of a response to the vision of God given to the Christian community, the church. They arise as a response to revelation. But what is this revelation? There are many people who ask, 'What is involved in being a Christian now? What must Christians believe?' Many traditional beliefs about Adam and Eve, the virgin birth, or the miracles may seem to be questioned or even abandoned by many theologians. And this may naturally lead to a fear that the Christian faith is in fact being undermined from within as well as from without, and that there will soon be nothing definite to keep hold of and proclaim. This is a natural fear, for it is a natural human desire to have some definite and simple propositions which can be clearly formulated and stated as the essence of one's belief. But it is important to see that this is a *fear*. That is, it is an anxiety which expresses reluctance to bring one's beliefs clearly into the light of criticism, lest they should fall. The existence of such a fear betrays the presence of a faith whose foundations are insecure; and often one conceals such insecurity by a show of intolerance, anger, and rejection of free critical inquiry. It is love which casts out fear; and if our lives are founded on God's love, we have nothing to fear from any inquiry. The faith which rests on love is calm and tolerant in the face of both inquiry and criticism; for it is based on a profound inner peace and security, which is never resentful, angry, or quarrelsome.

Moreover, although theoretical beliefs about the occurrence of miracles and so forth are not irrelevant to Christian faith, it is important to remember that it is not primarily these things which make the big practical difference to one's everday living as a Christian. Christian faith is not just a set of historical and metaphysical propositions, about which people may dispute from now to eternity. It is primarily the belief that reverence, penitence, and love are the proper attitudes to take to all human experience, and that we both learn more fully what these imply and learn to express them more fully as we come to the community of the church, in the companionship of those who seek those attitudes in their own lives. That is the basic and unchanging rock of Christian faith. Certainly, without it what may pass for faith is worthless. With it, one may believe many other things or take many sorts of view about the nature of the world and about difficult doctrines of atonement and Christology and so on; but one will possess the one thing needful, the heart and mind devoted to God in a real and practical way.

I hope it goes without saying that not all our opinions about these theoretical and rather abstruse matters can be equally true or reasonable. Nevertheless, if the stage comes when we get angry or quarrelsome or disputatious about such things, remember that we are then in danger of losing the one thing needful. We must hold fast to the truth; but that truth is not some intellectual formulation which we happen to prefer or believe; it is the way of life which increases reverence, penitence, and love in us, and which builds up the Christian community and does not divide it into quarrelsome factions.

What, then, must a Christian believe and stand by unshakeably? He must proclaim that the church is a community of people committed to exploring, by mutual help and encouragement, the way of creative love, of that fulfilment of self and creative response to reality which is found in reverence, penitence, and love. It does this in response to the disclosures of an ultimate meaning and value in the universe which have come in the Judaic tradition, and above all in the life and death and risen power of Jesus, the Christ. The church is a community of those who have been grasped by a vision of love and service expressed in the New Testament picture of Jesus. It is founded on the treasured memory of that man, and finds its life continually renewed and inspired by the living spiritual presence which is made known as it seeks to recall and make present the vision of God which was seen in the face of Jesus. Faith is the acceptance of a renewed life which comes to birth in the community which seeks to respond faithfully and fully to the vision of the divine love, calling, and purpose which was disclosed in Jesus.

I will end by returning to the contrast with which I began. Religious belief can be either restrictive, demonic, and neurotic; or it can be fulfilling, creative, and loving. These two possibilities are present in every form of religion; and we must be on constant guard that our faith is the latter. One finds restrictive religion where the community is exclusive and intolerant, imposing rigid rules on its members and harsh penalties or condemnation for those who deviate in any way; where the rites are treated as magical ways of obtaining one's requests, working automatically and without self-commitment; where prayer and piety become an entrance into a private fantasy-world of retreat and illusory security; and where creeds are strictly defined as the only permissible forms of beliefs, imposed intolerantly and adhered to uncritically.

For creative religion, faith is a creative response to that which discloses a meaningfulness and value in reality, and which evokes in one an irrevocable commitment to the attitudes which are felt to be appropriate responses to that reality. To have faith, to believe, is to enter the community of reverence, penitence, and love, which preserves in the Bible and liturgy the remembrance and celebration of those events which first brought the community into being and evoked those attitudes in men. For Christians, Jesus is the Lord, the man who discloses God to us and is our pattern for reconciling all life to God. He is the place where we discern man's ultimate purpose, the significance of our lives, and the demand to love without reservation. By relation to him we aim at fulfilment. But this does not mean that we are called to set ourselves up as the only people who have any spiritual truth. The final test of our faith is whether it does lead to a growth in love, trust, and hope. The Christian proclamation should be that here is a way of liberation from anxiety, greed, and fear. It is not for us to set limits around the elect and put ourselves inside and everyone else outside. The basic Christian demand to love and care for others, to seek the truth with sincerity and patience, entails that we must seek tolerant understanding of different views or interpretations than our own. There will always be those who remain unsure about what we take to be obvious. So what we can strive for is tolerance in matters of intellectual understanding, together with a total commitment to the love of God, revealed in Christ, offered to us in the community of the church.

Christian faith is, however, not just response to the vision of God in Christ. There must be the discipline of following the way of love; and there must be the response of the heart to the vision of God. But the Christian faith offers and demands more than these. It offers and demands a union with God himself, so that his love flows into our lives and is expressed through us in the world. As we turn to God more fully we find that the love with which we love God is transformed and replaced by God's own love, working in and through us, by which he loves himself. Our response is transfigured into unity. We are, as it were, taken up into the interior love of God, in the divine fellowship of the Trinity. We, being together in Christ, are taken up to live in God, to share in the life of God, and our love for God becomes indistinguishable from the love of God working in us. At this point we become aware that, even when we have mastered this part of the Christian way, even then we are standing merely on the foothills of Christian experience, and there are heights which stretch vastly higher beyond where we are. The ladder of contemplative and mystical prayer stands yet before us; and we can see those who have begun to climb and hear their testimony of a deeper union with the being of Christ and an indwelling of Christ in the heart, until their lives are completely hid with Christ in God, and the living Christ transfigures their lives totally from within. Such fulness of love and delight in God is the work of grace, the free gift of God's friendship; it is something for us continually to seek and pray for, by turning to God in faith and hope. It comes by his gift, as we are recreated in Christ, and as our beings are transfigured by the love which we contemplate in Christ. In the end, human fulfilment comes as God unites us to himself eternally, and we are made one in Christ, are raised up to share in his own limitless love.

We, most of us ordinary folk, may look with love

and longing to that deep and inward union which is the crown of the Christian way. But for most of us even the foothills are almost as exhausting as they are exhilarating, and we may be grateful that God has opened up the Christian way to us also, by freely giving us his friendship and love and drawing us into a deeper appreciation of reverence, penitence, and love within the fellowship of his church. This Christian way is our vocation; this is the pattern of true, enduring human fulfilment.

LORD JESUS,
in your life we see the vision of the love of God;
through you we hear God's call to respond to him in
love; we are upheld and empowered by your Spirit
and given a share in the eternal life of God;
>help us to hold firm to this vision,
>to be always open to your call,
>to live in our lives the pattern of your life,
>and to strive for perfect union with you.

Lord, we are healed by your life, offered for us;
>by our union with you, we offer our lives for the
>healing of the world;
>by your love, you create us a people for yourself,
>holy and dedicated to God;
>you offer your people to the Father in union with
>yourself;
so, as we embrace your self-offering for us, we ourselves are offered with you and given back to live for
others through your power.

So, Lord, transfigure us with your love, and through
our prayers bring us and all men to the perfect vision
of God in the community of all God's people.